100 Questions and Answers about Sikh Americans

The beliefs behind
the articles of faith

D1528139

Michigan State University
School of Journalism

Front Edge Publishing

For more information and further discussion, visit

news.jrn.msu.edu/culturalcompetence/

Cover design and illustration by Rick Nease
www.RickNeaseArt.com

Published by
Front Edge Publishing
42807 Ford Road, No. 234
Canton, MI, 48187

Front Edge Publishing books are available for discount bulk purchases for events, corporate use and small groups. Special editions, including books with corporate logos, personalized covers and customized interiors, are available for purchase. For more information, contact Front Edge Publishing at info@FrontEdgePublishing.com.

Contents

The Bias Busters team dedicates this guide to the Sikh and Indianapolis communities, which lost eight people in an attack on a FedEx warehouse on April 16, 2021.

In memory of:

Matthew R. Alexander, 32
Samaria Blackwell, 19
Amarjeet Johal, 66
Jasvinder Kaur, 50
Amarjit Sekhon, 48
Jaswinder Singh, 68
Karli Smith, 19
John Weisert, 74

Acknowledgments

This guide was created by these Michigan State University students:

Top row: Ellen Taylor Bartush, Bridgette Bauer, Emily Jeanne Bevard, Subah Bhatia

Second row: Dea Chappell, Reanu Miriam Charles, Ryan Joseph Collins, Kennedi Mnaya Dubose

Third row: Kendall Marie Gulau, Megan Nalazek, Rachael Nemic, Elena Shklyar

Fourth row: Kaylee Heeju Uh, Akshita Verma, Bryson D. Watkins, Sam Woznicki

Bottom: Jiamian Zhu

Zhu took the photographs in this guide at the Sikh Gurdwara in Rochester Hills, Michigan. Adrian Kresnak and Chloe Peter, who worked on previous Bias Busters guides, also have contributions in this guide. Michigan State students under the direction of Design Artist-in-Residence

Richard Epps made the graphics, and their work is credited individually. Dina Kaur and Lacie Kunselman helped with final editing.

We could not do this work without helpful allies. We were advised by Sikhs who are generous with their time and live the Sikh value of seva, selfless service.

Several organizations partnered with us to make this guide a success. They include: The Sikh Coalition, SALDEF, Sikhs United and the InterFaith Leadership Council of Metropolitan Detroit. We relied heavily on SALDEF's 2020 National Sikh American Survey, an opt-in study with about 2,000 respondents.

Guest lecturers included:

Raman Singh, president of the InterFaith Leadership Council of Metropolitan Detroit. She volunteers with the Women's Interfaith Solutions for Dialogue and Outreach in Metro Detroit, World Sabbath and the Michigan Roundtable for Diversity and Inclusion. She is a board member of the Detroit area's Gurdwara Sahib Mata Tripta.

Kiran Kaur Gill is executive director of the Sikh American Legal Defense and Education Fund, or SALDEF. She is former president and CEO of PARS Environmental, Inc., an environmental consulting firm based in Robbinsville, New Jersey. Additionally, she has been a long-time adviser and volunteer for SALDEF, playing a critical role in the expansion of its Law Enforcement Partnership Program and the expansion of the SikhLEAD Internship to New Jersey.

Others from SALDEF who provided help were Board Member **Amman Singh Seehra** and fellow **Ikaasa Suri**.

Several members of the Michigan State University Sikh Students Association, led by officers **Kajalpreet Kaur**, **Jasleen Kaur** and **Arshveen Rathod**, also visited to suggest and answer questions and read drafts. Association members were among the many interviewed for the guide.

Allies who provided guidance or who reviewed content include Sikh Coalition Education Director **Pritpal Kaur** and legal client and community services manager **Assees Kaur**.

We would also like to thank InterFaith Leadership Council of Metropolitan Detroit's **Imaan Singh** and **Wendy Miller Gamer**, director of programs and the IFLC's Religious Diversity Journeys.

Tejkiran Singh of the Sikh Gurdwara in Rochester Hills, Michigan, helped arrange photography.

Finally, thanks to MSU School of Journalism professor and director **Dr. Tim P. Vos** for his support of this series.

Foreword

By Sharan Kaur Singh

Sikhs have lived in the United States for over a century, but many Americans still have limited information about the Sikh American community. To gain a deeper understanding of who Sikhs are, it is imperative that one recognizes the origins of Sikhs, appreciates the Sikh beliefs and understands the significance of the Sikh identity. These include the role Sikh women play in society and the values that Sikhs practice on a daily basis. Sikhs promote justice, peace and civil rights. Despite Sikhs being persecuted since the religion was founded, Sikhism is a defender of all faiths, and its core tenet is to serve humankind.

As a national Sikh American organization, SALDEF works to raise Sikh awareness, build dialogue and deepen understanding. We are deeply appreciative of this publication by these Michigan State students. By asking and answering questions on the Sikh faith in a straightforward and easy-to-read manner, it will help promote interfaith communication and be an invaluable resource for the community.

Sharan Kaur Singh is a program director with SALDEF. She does advocacy work including conducting cultural awareness training for government officials, law enforcement, FBI and TSA officers as part of SALDEF's national speakers bureau. She oversees SikhLEAD, a national Sikh youth legislative internship and leadership program that encourages civic engagement. She is on advisory groups for federal and state agencies including the FBI WFO Multi-Cultural Engagement Council and HACCEN (HAte Crimes Community ENgagement working Group).

Introduction

By Simran Jeet Singh

Despite being the fifth-largest organized religion in the world, Sikhi (westernized as Sikhism) is often misunderstood — especially among American audiences. Sikhs have been underrepresented in popular and news media, though Sikhs have been part of American history and culture for more than 125 years, with roughly half a million Sikhs in the United States. A basic familiarity with Sikh history, culture and values — as well as core tenets and practices, from concepts like seva and chardi kala to the five Sikh articles of faith — is an essential foundation for responsible and respectful understanding of this dynamic, multifaceted community.

Dr. Simran Jeet Singh is an educator, writer, activist and scholar who speaks regularly on issues of diversity, inclusion and equity. He is based at Union Seminary and is senior fellow with the Sikh Coalition. He's the first Sikh wire-service columnist in U.S. history. He is the author of "Fauja Singh Keeps Going: The True Story of the Oldest Person to Run a Marathon," the first children's book from a major publisher to center on a Sikh story. His latest book is "The Light We Give: How Sikh Wisdom Can Transform Your Life."

Preface

Working on "100 Questions and Answers About Sikh Americans" was a challenge and an honor for our Michigan State University journalism class. We had the interest but little knowledge about Sikhs. Some of our authors had Sikh friends but had never talked with them about their faith. We reached out and asked Sikhs what questions they thought should be included.

We learned that, despite their long history in the United States, Sikhs seldom get to frame their own story. Often, they are ignored until an event that originates outside their community calls attention to them. These events are often attacks on their lives or their rights. When a people's story is framed this way, they are inevitably cast in a defensive role. They are not asked about their values and principles but are associated with and asked to react to negative events not of their making.

The stories Sikh Americans would like to tell are about their relationship with God and humanity, their values and their contributions. We worked with Sikh Americans to answer some of the basic, everyday questions non-Sikhs have but might not find the opportunity to ask. Our plan was to put core beliefs and values ahead of headline-grabbing practices and challenges.

At the end of our project, the Bias Busters team felt we had something that could help people know Sikh Americans better.

Four days before our final class, a gunman attacked the FedEx center in Indianapolis, killing eight people. Four were Sikhs. Our new allies were grievously wounded by the attack, which echoed so many of their struggles. Once again, they were in the headlines for something that happened to them but that was not about them. Their identities and values did not make the headlines.

The Associated Press story quoted Satjeet Kaur, executive director of the Sikh Coalition: "We are time and time again disproportionately facing senseless and often very targeted attacks. … The impact on the community is traumatic, not just particularly the families that face the senseless violence, but also in the community at large because it's community trauma."

The students asked to dedicate this guide to the Sikh and Indianapolis communities, and we sought consent from our allies.

Joe Grimm
Series editor
Bias Busters
Michigan State University School of Journalism

Origins

1 When was Sikhi founded?

Sikhism was founded in 1469 in the Common Era. Sikhi, as the religion is called by the people who practice it, is more than 550 years old. It is the youngest of the world's five largest organized religions.

2 What is the correct way to say "Sikh?"

According to the World Sikh Council, "Sikh" is pronounced "sick." The plural "Sikhs" is pronounced like "six." While pronouncing the word as "sick" is the original, authentic pronunciation, many people, even some Sikhs, pronounce it as "seek."

3 Where did the religion originate?

Sikhism originated in Punjab, a region now split by the border of India and Pakistan. The region, a little smaller than West Virginia, was divided between India and Pakistan during the 1947 Partition of British India. This forced the Sikh population in the Pakistan regions to undertake arduous journeys to India almost overnight. People in both countries were displaced. Sikhs see this as one of the largest and deadliest migrations in history. Now, the vast majority of Sikhs live in Punjab, India.

4 Who started the religion?

Sikhism was founded by Guru Nanak Dev in a small Punjabi village. He created a religion very different from the area's two dominating faiths, Hinduism and Islam. He did not identify with their rituals. He saw merit in meditation, simplistic worship, disavowing the caste system and doing good in society. Sikhi teachings were carried on by nine gurus after Guru Nanak. The tenth and final human guru, Guru Gobind Singh, completed the Guru Granth Sahib. This is the holy text for Sikhism and is the 11th and enduring guru.

5 Who are the 11 gurus of Sikhism?

From 1469 to 1708, there were 10 living gurus:

Guru Nanak, the first human guru, traveled widely and opposed the caste system.

Guru Angad, founder of many schools, advocated for physical and religious exercises.

Guru Amar Das also opposed the caste system and founded free kitchens.

Guru Ram Das founded the city of Amritsar and Darbar Sahib, popularly known as the Golden Temple, the holiest of several Sikh pilgrimage sites in Punjab, India.

Guru Arjan compiled the scriptures of the Sikhs and was the first guru to be martyred.

Guru Hargobind taught the importance of spiritual (piri) and temporal (miri) power. He also stressed the importance of defending the faith and the weak through the concept of the saint-soldier.

Guru Har Rai formalized the tradition of dasvandh, contributing a tenth of one's income toward charitable causes. He also administered a system of "masands" to organize and be responsible for local Sikh communities.

Guru Har Krishan became the youngest guru at age 5. He is known for helping those who were physically ill, particularly during a smallpox epidemic.

Guru Tegh Bahadur championed freedom of worship and defended the rights of Kashmiri Pandits, who were Hindus, even though it cost him his own life. He founded the city of Anandpur.

Guru Gobind Singh established the Khalsa Panth (the community of initiated Sikhs) and the articles of faith. Shortly before his death in 1708, he declared the Guru Granth Sahib his continuing successor.

Guru Granth Sahib is the scripture of the Sikhs and much more than a holy text. It is present at all Sikh services and is the eternal guru. Sikhi's truths are embodied in the Guru Granth Sahib. The text includes 1,430 pages of spiritual hymns organized in raags, frameworks of North Indian classical music, that can be sung. Adi Granth refers to the earlier unfinished, unpublished draft.

Beliefs

6 What is Sikhi?

"Sikhi," known by many Westerners as Sikhism, is the religion, a path of learning. A "Sikh" is a disciple, student or learner. Sikhs pursue salvation through the message of God as revealed by the gurus, which promotes prayer and selfless service. Sikhs believe in one God who created the universe. All beings are equal and a part of this entity. Sikhism rejects discrimination based on gender, creed or social standing.

7 How do Sikhs view other religions?

Given their belief that all people are part of the same universal presence, Sikhs are very accepting of other religions. They do not think of their religion as the truth or the only one. They do not seek converts to gain followers.

8 How was the Guru Granth Sahib compiled?

This document contains writings by the faith's gurus. It also includes verses by Hindu and Muslim saints. Its primary writers were the first five gurus and the ninth. The Sikh gurus compiled the writings themselves. The Guru Granth Sahib Ji is held as the highest authority in the religion, and it is the centerpiece of all gurdwaras (Sikh houses of worship). Although much of the scripture is influenced by Punjabi, it includes several other languages such as Sanskrit, Sindhi, Gujarati, Marathi, Hindi, Arabic and Persian. It is the only major religious text compiled during the life of its writers. The languages in the scripture are written in the Gurmukhī script. All copies of the Guru Granth Sahib are identical.

9 What are the core tenets of Sikh living?

Sikhism stands on three pillars. The first is Kirt Karna, which means humble living. The second pillar, Nam Japna, stands for focusing on God. The third, Vand Chhakna, stands for sharing with the community and those less fortunate. Sikhs live a life dedicated to God and the community. In Sikhism, all people of all religions are equal. The religion focuses on finding genuine, divine love and oneness in every aspect of life.

10 Do Sikhs believe in an afterlife?

Sikhs focus on doing good for others and honoring God in this life, rather than focusing on what comes next. They are not here to make amends for previous lives or to attain rewards later. Sikhism teaches that one's spiritual union with God and the universe is achieved by serving humanity and avoiding maya. Maya is the part of our reality that takes us from serving humanity. Its components include greed, anger, ego, attachment and lust. These are known as the "five thieves."

11 Do Sikhs believe in reincarnation?

Sikhism follows the idea of reincarnation, meaning people have earlier lives as well as an afterlife. Individuals are born, live a full life and then are reborn. Sikhism teaches that this life on Earth is simply one part of a cycle. They leave the cycle when they truly become one with God.

12 Do Sikhs believe in heaven and hell?

Sikhs are taught to focus on their actions and deeds in this lifetime, not notions of heaven and hell. The Guru Granth Sahib asks Sikhs to make the best of their time on Earth. This is their opportunity to connect with Waheguru — the one God. That name means wonderful teacher or guru. Sikhs believe in karma, which takes into account good and bad actions. The person is then rewarded or must endure consequences based on their deeds.

13 How do Sikhs view God?

Sikhs believe in one eternal God who created all things. God's essence cannot be described. God is genderless and formless. God is eternal, compassionate, fearless, self-sufficient and has no enemies. The Guru Granth Sahib begins with a statement called the Mool Mantar. It contains the central beliefs about Waheguru. It opens with the declaration "Ik Onkar," meaning "There is only one God, the Creator." The declaration says that everything in the universe, including God and people, share a oneness and that all are equal.

Identity

14 How is Sikhism distinct from other religions?

Guru Nanak proclaimed a unique religion as he established Sikhi. After a revelation, he said, "There is neither Hindu nor Muslim, so whose path shall I follow? I shall follow God's path. God is neither Hindu nor Muslim, and the path I follow is God's." Sikhi is a religion with its own values, teachings, houses of worship and scripture. It does not hold itself or any religion above others and sees everyone as equal parts of the same oneness.

15 Why do many Sikhs share the same last names?

The gurus instructed Sikhs to use surnames that simultaneously reflect equality among members and distinction from other religions. Having the name Singh or Kaur indicates membership in the Khalsa. All Sikhs were given the last name Singh or Kaur on March 30, 1699. Sikhs celebrate the formation of the Khalsa on March 30 through a celebration called Vaisakhi. The surname for males is Singh, meaning lion, signifying bravery and leadership. For females the surname is Kaur. It means princess and signifies independence and nobility. Using just two last names for everyone rejected castes and placed followers from different social and economic backgrounds on equal footing. Some Sikhs use a family surname and have Singh or Kaur as their middle name. You might also encounter other words in names. Sahib and Ji connote respect. Dev, which means God, and Ji are used in reference to the Sikh gurus.

16 Do spouses and siblings have different surnames?

Many spouses and siblings have different surnames. Many women use Kaur instead of adopting family names from marriage. This represents them as independent and valuable outside of their relationship with a man. When a child is born, Kaur or Singh may be added to a chosen name and a family name. So, siblings of different genders and spouses may have different surnames.

17 Did Sikhism challenge the caste system?

Since its origin, Sikhi rejected the rigid social hierarchy of castes. The first guru set castes aside. The concept of oneness, shared names, free communal meals at all gurdwaras, and turbans reflect equality.

Women have been championed since the first guru.

18 What is the role of women in Sikhism?

From the beginning, Sikhi has been based on gender equality. It maintains a deep-seated belief that men and women are equal in all facets of life. Guru Nanak, the founder of Sikhism, asserted from the beginning that women were equal to men and must be treated as such. He worked to uplift the status of women in society by encouraging them to participate in all facets of religious and social community and practice. He wrote, "We are born of woman, we are conceived in the womb of woman, we are engaged and married to woman. We make friendship with woman and the lineage continued because of woman. When one woman dies, we take another one, we are bound with the world through woman. Why should we talk ill of her, who gives birth to kings? The woman is born from woman; there is none without her. Only the One True Lord is without woman." The gurus also abolished the Hindu practice where a widow was expected to take her life on her husband's funeral pyre.

19 How is gender equality demonstrated?

The Guru Granth Sahib explicitly condemns practices that subjugate women. These include female infanticide, asserting authority over women captured in war, and stigma around widows remarrying. Sikh women do not have to take their husband's last name upon marriage. They have equality in property rights, participation in society and religious worship.

20 May Sikh women dress and act as they wish?

Since the religion's foundation, women have participated in the same cultural, religious and political activities as men. They keep the articles of faith. Traditionally, Sikh women cover their heads with a turban or scarf, but this is optional.

21 Does Sikhism have a central authority?

No primary person, council or place governs Sikhism. The ultimate source remains the eternal Guru Granth Sahib, the religious text. Guru Gobind Singh, the tenth Guru, also vested authority in the Khalsa Panth, the collective community of practicing Sikhs. India has five places, called takhts, that Sikhs look to for guidance. Takhts are historically and religiously significant gurdwaras. Three are in Punjab and two are in other parts of India. A sixth takht has been proposed at Guru Nanak's birthplace in present-day Pakistan. Occasionally, takhts issue decrees, called hukamnamas, on issues. Besides referring to these seats of influence, the word takht means the throne on which the Guru Granth Sahib rests in a gurdwara.

22 Is Sikhism a culture?

Sikhism is a religion, not a culture or ethnicity. The religion is often accompanied by cultural elements in terms of local practices for food, celebration and traditions. Most Sikhs have Indian, Pakistani and Punjabi origins and observe practices of those cultures.

23 How does culture differ among Sikhs?

Sikhism is practiced in cultures all around the world. While religion and culture co-exist, one does not dictate the principles of the other. It is important when learning about Sikh people to ask which of their practices are religious, which are cultural and even which are generational.

Values

24 What values are most important to Sikh people?

Core values rest in the belief in one God who resides in the heart of every human being. Sikhs value equality, selfless service, living truthfully and upholding social justice. These are practiced by always remembering God, earning a humble living honestly and performing selfless service, or seva.

25 What is seva?

Pronounced SAY-vah, Sikhs believe these actions cultivate humility, which helps them connect with the divine. This applies to acts done for Sikhs and non-Sikhs alike. Seva is offered without expectation of reward in this life or later lives.

26 How do Sikhs perform seva?

Sikhs perform acts of service by helping the community. It can occur in many forms anywhere and at any time. Seva is a regular part of life in places of worship. Actions include preparing and serving free meals to the community, cleaning dishes, cleaning the shoes of worshippers and maintaining the premises.

27 Are Sikhs involved in volunteerism?

The larger community sees seva most keenly at times of crisis, natural disaster and holidays. During the COVID-19 pandemic, the Delhi Sikh Gurdwara Management Committee helped feed more than 1.5 million hungry people in India. It sent trucks filled with food to remote places and set up free ambulance services. In the United States, Sikhs often organize or participate in holiday food drives.

28 Is there a Sikh philosophy?

Sikhs maintain an optimistic and positive mindset often expressed as "rising spirit." This blissful mental state is rooted in the belief that God is merciful and without enemies. Accepting God's will, even when tested by hard times, protects and benefits God's creations. This spirit is called chardi kala.

Articles of Faith

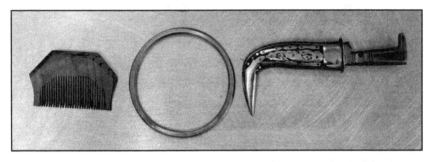

The khanga, kara and kirpan, three of the articles of faith.

29 What are the Five Ks?

These are called kakaars, or the articles of faith. According to the Sikh Coalition, "Sikhs cherish their articles of faith primarily because they see them as a gift from their beloved guru. Trying to understand these articles solely on the basis of their function is missing the point."

The Five Ks for men and women are:

Kesh: Uncut hair. To maintain this, men and some women wear a turban, a related article of faith called a dastar. There are many varieties of hair coverings. While turbans are one of the most visible signs of Sikh identity, kesh is uncut hair, not the covering.

Kangha: A small wooden comb to keep the hair tidy.

Kara: An iron or steel bracelet. It reminds Sikhs to behave ethically. Its circular shape is a reminder of continuity.

Kachera: A cotton undergarment resembling knee-length shorts. It reflects dignity, modesty and high moral character.

Kirpan: A small sword or dagger. This represents a Sikh's duty to seek justice and fight oppression of any people. It represents defense and upholding values, not aggression or revenge.

30 What is the significance of uncut hair?

It is a sign of accepting God's will. This practice dates back to the first guru, Guru Nanak. Maintaining this article shows identity and history. This is known as the seal of the gurus. It is a sign of respect for all of God's creations.

31 Is uncut hair mandatory?

Sikhism is a diverse religion. Sikhs can be initiated into the Khalsa, the community, or not. Each Sikh decides how closely to keep the articles of faith. Some Sikhs choose to cut their hair as some jobs require it. But they are still Sikh.

32 Is this why Sikhs wear turbans?

The dastar or turban is an article of faith in itself, connected as it is to kesh. Turbans give Sikhs their unique visible identity and spiritual strength. They also make them accountable for helping others and upholding Sikh values. Turbans, like crowns, signify the people who wear them are unique, noble and command respect.

33 How is the Sikh turban different from other head coverings?

Turbans may be found in other cultures or traditions, but for Sikhs they are an article of faith and, for initiated Sikhs, a religious requirement. There are many styles of turban, and even Sikhs do not have just one style. They are wrapped on from a long piece of cloth and are tied in different ways. Turbans come in a rainbow of colors and patterns. Colors can have significance, and people may choose colors for personal taste or special occasions. For Sikhs, a turban is a religious article tied on every day and not a fashion accessory or a hat which is taken on and off. The turban must never be touched without permission. It should not be forcibly removed.

Worship

The Guru Granth Sahib being fanned with a chaur sahib. The symbol in the foreground is the khanda.

34 What is a Sikh house of worship called?

Sikhs come together for congregational worship in a building called a gurdwara. That means "the gateway to the guru."

35 What is the interior focal point?

The focal point inside the gurdwara is the Guru Granth Sahib. The sacred scripture is in the prayer hall, or diwan. It is on a platform or throne called a takht or manji sahib.

The scripture is under a structure called a palki with a canopy called a chanani above. The Guru Granth Sahib is covered with beautiful pieces of cloth called rumallas. Sikhs bow to the Guru Granth Sahib, and it is fanned with a chaur sahib. This is traditionally a wooden or metal handle with yak hair attached to it. The fanning symbolizes reverence for the scripture's content. When a copy of the Guru Granth Sahib must be discarded, a funerary service is performed.

36 What are a gurdwara's external features?

The traditional design of the pre-eminent gurdwara in Amritsar, Punjab, India, has four doors to symbolize that people from every point of the compass are welcome. Many gurdwaras also fly a flag called the Nishan Sahib. It signifies that this is a Sikh house of worship and that all are welcome. The Nishan Sahib is normally yellow/orange and blue, bearing the Sikh khanda.

37 What is the khanda?

This symbol, dating to the 1930s, represents belief in one God. It reflects fundamental concepts of Sikhism such as divine justice. The symbol has a double-edged sword, a circle called the chakar and two curved swords called kirpans. The khanda appears on the cover of this guide.

Rumalla cloths are used to cover the Guru Granth Sahib.

38 Why is food served at a gurdwara?

The institution of langar refers to the food prepared and served as part of this tradition. The dining area is called the langar or langar hall. Food is served by volunteers and prepared for free in a community kitchen. It promotes equality and hospitality. The meal is simple vegetarian food so all may join, no matter their diet. Langar typically consists of Punjabi food such as bread (roti), lentils (daal), vegetable dishes and dessert. Everyone eats together at ground level to reinforce the belief in equality.

39 Do men and women sit separately in the gurdwara?

Often, men and women sit on separate sides of the hall during the service to avoid distractions. It is not a religious requirement. It is done out of cultural consideration.

Gender separation is not a strictly enforced rule nor is it practiced in every gurdwara. In the COVID-19 pandemic, for example, some gurdwaras adjusted placement to achieve social distancing and to allow families to sit together.

40 Do men and women have different roles in the gurdwara?

Sikh teachings are clear that, in the gurdwara, women and men may play equal roles, although in practice, women are still sometimes less represented on committees. Fewer women lead in congregational settings, too, although full participation of women in all aspects of the gurdwara is increasingly encouraged. Public worship can be run by men or women. Notably, women play key roles in other aspects of public Sikh engagement. They lead several national Sikh organizations.

41 What is proper etiquette in a gurdwara?

The gurdwara is designed to be open and inclusive. Guests are always welcome. People who enter the gurdwara should remove their shoes, wash their hands and cover their heads. It should be clear where to place shoes. The gurdwara may be large and formal or in a converted home. Members usually sit on the floor, facing the Guru Granth Sahib, typically with their legs crossed. They do not expose the soles of their feet to the Guru Granth Sahib out of respect. There is singing of verses from the sacred scriptures, communal prayers, readings and talks on

Overnight, the Guru Granth Sahib reposes
in a room called the sach khand.

spiritual topics. Spoken parts may be delivered in Punjabi and translated into English. Donations may be made if there is a collection or offering box.

42 Who maintains the gurdwara?

There is no official clergy or priesthood in Sikhism. Some gurdwaras task a granthi versed in reading the scriptures with responsibilities relating to worship. A granthi's responsibilities include arranging services and ceremonially opening and closing the Guru Granth Sahib each day. The granthi might also lead the akhand path at times of mourning and celebration. The akhand path is the continual recitation of the Guru Granth Sahib. This takes 48 hours. Any practicing Sikh may perform these duties, and many Sikhs perform these duties on their own. Gurdwara finances, events and maintenance are typically overseen by a council selected from the sangat or congregation.

Prayer

43 How do Sikhs worship in the gurdwara?

Prayer revolves around the Guru Granth Sahib. Sikhs participate in kirtan, which means "singing the praises of God." The hymns sung during kirtan, called shabads, are contained in the Guru Granth Sahib and are set to traditional frameworks of notes. These complex scales are called raags or ragas and are meant to elicit certain feelings. Sikhs do not have ordained clergy, so any devout Sikh can lead prayers or kirtan.

44 Is Sikh prayer a form of meditation?

Singing shabads and reciting prayer helps Sikhs meditate on God's name, carry it with them daily and remember to praise God throughout the week. Sikh meditation and prayer take place every day. They can take place at home or at a gurdwara.

45 What language is the service in?

Punjabi is typical, though there may be lectures or short translations in English. Some gurdwaras offer services in English for people who do not read Gurmukhī, the written language of the scriptures.

46 Are there certain days people go to the gurdwara?

Gurdwaras in Punjab are typically open around the clock every day. No day is holier than another. However, gurdwaras in the diaspora typically hold weekend services, when most members in their countries are free from work. Gurdwara attendants can keep them open all day or have morning and evening worship.

47 How do Sikhs practice at home?

Sikhs worship at home by saying, singing, repeating and listening to prayers. Initiated Sikhs pray a minimum of three times a day — in the morning, in the evening and before sleeping. Some Sikhs run prayer beads, called mala, through their fingers as they repeat and contemplate God's name, Waheguru. Many Sikhs read compilations of prayers from the Guru Granth Sahib. These smaller books are called pothis or gutkas and are common in Sikh households.

The khanda can be seen on this gurdwara's ceiling.

48 What is a typical prayer?

The first verse in the Guru Granth Sahib is The Mool
Mantar. This, coupled with the word "Waheguru"
(Gurmantar) from Guru Gobind Singh, comprises the
foundation of "Naam" (God's Name) for Sikhs. Sikhs
believe the Mool Mantar is Guru Nanak's first teaching. It
sums up Sikhs' central beliefs about God and is reflected in
the Ik Onkar. The English translation of the verse is:

There is only one God.

God's name is eternal truth.

God is the creator who is pervading in everything.

God is without fear and is all bliss.

God is without hate or enmity.

God is beyond time, space, form and features.

God is beyond birth and death and is self-manifested and self-existent.

Oneness with the one truth is realized with the grace of the true guru.

The declaration means everything in the universe, including God and people, share a oneness and all are equal. Ik Onkar means there is an absolute unity among all beings. It projects a monotheistic image of God.

Ik Onkar

Practices

49 Do Sikhs follow dietary restrictions?

Sikhs have many different dietary practices. The code of conduct encourages Sikhs to not eat meat butchered in ritualistic ways, as is done under halal rules. There are wide interpretations of this. Some Sikhs do not eat meat at all. Some avoid beef or pork out of consideration for restrictions on neighboring Hindu and Muslim religions. Some avoid all animal products, eggs, fish and sometimes dairy.

50 Are there typical foods for Sikhs?

For many Sikhs, food follows culture rather than religious doctrine. Punjab, known as the "Land of Five Rivers" for tributaries of the Indus River, is a fertile land where dairy production flourishes. Many Punjabi dishes are rich and creamy. Some are made with an Indian cheese called paneer. Lentils (daal) are a common ingredient in Punjabi food. Rice and flatbreads are staples. A Punjabi dessert is jalebi, a fried, orange, syrupy pretzel similar to a funnel cake.

51 Can one convert to Sikhism?

Yes, but Sikhs do not actively seek conversions. For those who wish to become initiated, there is a ceremony called the amrit sanchar. Once initiated, the person is said to join the Khalsa community of Sikhs. In becoming a Sikh, people pledge to live according to Sikh teachings as best as possible. This includes wearing the articles of faith and using Singh or Kaur as a last name. Conversion might precede a non-Sikh's marriage to a Sikh partner.

52 Does one have to be Punjabi, Indian or South Asian to be Sikh?

No, there is no racial, ancestral or cultural requirement to being Sikh.

53 Is there a Sikh code of conduct?

The Sikh code of conduct is the Rehat Maryada. The code has rules for internal and external conduct. The internal code is to live an honest, spiritual life. The external code is to live a visibly ethical and righteous life. It states that a Sikh must practice bani, the concept of spiritual life, and bana, the doctrine of wearing the articles of faith. The Rehat Maryada is positive, not punitive. It encourages devotion to God's will.

54 What is the Sikh salutation or greeting?

Sikhs often greet each other with "Sat sri akaal." That means "God is truth" or "Truth is eternal." A longer greeting is "Waheguru Ji ka Khalsa Waheguru Ji kee fateh." That is, "the community belongs to God and all victory belongs to God." It is perfectly acceptable to greet Sikhs in the customary expressions of their daily language as you would greet anyone else.

55 Why are there no Sikh clergy members?

Sikhism does not have religious leaders in the way many religions do. The belief is that each individual is free to cultivate their own relationship with the divine. At one point a priest-like role developed, known as masands, but this was eliminated after complaints of corruption. Today, any devout Sikh can read scripture during a service and perform the rites of worship.

56 What role does music play?

Music, particularly North Indian classical music, is integral to the Sikh religion, given that the sacred scripture is organized in melodic raags. Music accompanies many worship ceremonies. Instruments include the tabla (hand drums) and the harmonium, a reed organ in which air blowing over reeds produces notes. Sikhs also accompany kirtan on stringed instruments, such as the taus. It is played with a bow and is attributed to Guru Gobind Singh.

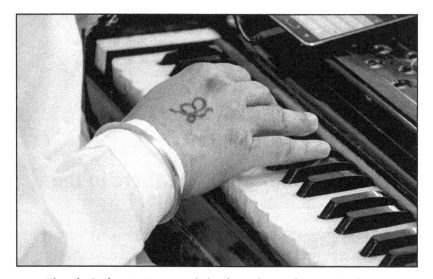

The Ik Onkar tattoo and the kara bracelet remind
this harmonium player of his faith.

57 Does Sikhism have branches?

Not really. Belief in the Guru Granth Sahib Ji, prayers and
religious practices are consistent. Historically, there were
disagreements about the succession of gurus or issues
of orthodoxy. In the United States, Sikh Dharma was
founded in the 1970s by Harbhajan Singh. This stream is
mostly White American converts who focus on disciplined
mediation.

Demographics

58 How many Sikhs are there in the world?

Multiple sources estimate there are 25 million Sikhs in the world. This makes it the fifth largest organized religion on the globe after Christianity, Islam, Buddhism and Hinduism. Sikhs live throughout Asia and in Australia/ Oceania, North America and the United Kingdom. There are also sizable Sikh communities in Malaysia and Singapore.

59 Are most Sikhs in India?

Yes. Although Sikhs live throughout the world, they are a religious minority in every country where they live. After India, countries with the largest Sikh populations include Canada, the United States and the United Kingdom.

60 What languages do Sikhs speak?

Sikhs typically speak the native languages of the places where they live, as well as Punjabi. More than 80 million people around the world speak Punjabi. Like English, it is written from left to right. Punjabi is often written in the Gurmukhī script, an alphabet developed by the Sikh Gurus themselves. The Gurmukhī alphabet has 35 characters. Just as some gurdwaras have services in English, some teach Punjabi.

U.S. Sikhs

61 How many Sikhs live in the United States?

Sikh organizations estimate at least 500,000-700,000 Sikhs live in the United States. Pew Research data drawn from Census figures about Asian Americans indicate there are at least 200,000 American Sikhs across all age groups. About 5.5 percent of U.S. adults identify as Asian American. About 1 percent of them identify as Sikh. However, not all Sikhs are of Asian origin.

62 Does the U.S. Census Bureau count Sikhs?

The bureau changes the way it counts every time it runs, once each decade. As for Sikhs, around 1900, the U.S. census counted Sikhs as Hindus. At the time Sikh immigrants outnumbered Hindus but were mislabeled. Their larger numbers were owed to the fact that most early South Asian immigrants came from Punjab. The 2020 U.S. Census long form was the first to recognize Sikhs in their own category. While there was not a separate Sikh checkbox, it could be written under race. This was to be counted as a distinct group under "Asian" rather than as "Asian Indian" as had been done previously.

63 When did Sikhs first come to the United States?

Sikhs came to the United States more than 130 years ago in the late 1880s. When Punjabi immigration to the United States began in 1901-1910, most of those 5,762 immigrants arriving in Northern California were Sikhs. A 1908 amendment to Canada's Immigration Act prevented Indians from entering that country. This redirected several thousand Sikhs to the Pacific coast of the United States. In this first decade, about 85-90 percent of Punjabi immigrants were Sikh. The United States later excluded Asians from immigration. Those restrictions were eased in 1952 and 1965. Today, the proportion of people who are Sikh is higher in Canada than it is in the United States.

64 What were historic Sikh contributions to the United States?

In the early years, many Sikhs helped build the transcontinental railroad in the West. Other early arrivals found work on California farms and Pacific Northwestern lumber mills. The first U.S. gurdwara was established in 1912 in Stockton, California. Other Sikhs served the United States in world wars. Sikh-American physicist Narinder Singh Kapany is credited with inventing fiber optics. In 1957, Dalip Singh Saund became the first Asian American elected to the U.S. Congress.

65 Where are the religion's U.S. population centers today?

The major concentrations are in New York City, New Jersey and Connecticut, in California and along the coasts. There are approximately 300 gurdwaras throughout the United States.

66 Do U.S. Sikhs feel included in society?

Although Sikhs have been in the United States for nearly 150 years, many other Americans know little about them. Many Sikh Americans say they feel alienated by a lack of representation in news media, film and TV. Since their arrival, many have met discrimination. Some attacks followed the Sept. 11, 2001, terror attacks, although Sikhs had nothing to do with them. Many Americans saw Sikhs' visible identity — including their turbans, beards, and brown skin — and wrongly associated them with terrorism. Organizations including the Sikh Coalition and SALDEF work to have Sikhs recognized as equal citizens.

U.S. Sikhs' feelings of acceptance

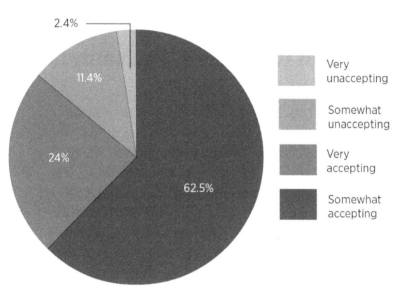

2.4%

11.4%

24%

62.5%

Very unaccepting

Somewhat unaccepting

Very accepting

Somewhat accepting

Source: National Sikh American Survey

Graphic by Omari Sadiq

Families and Children

67 What is the role of the family in Sikhism?

The life of a householder and the importance of the family have been promoted since the time of the religion's founder, Guru Nanak. The gurus taught that the family unit and procreation are essential to a healthy society. Sikhi values of honor and modesty play strong roles in family relationships. Many teachings encourage Sikhs to live as a family, to raise children and to be active community members. Sikhi's teachings focus on parental duties and nurturing and protecting children. Elders are held in high regard.

68 Are there gender roles within families?

Sikhism highlights spiritual equality between men and women, though members may play different roles depending on the family. Traditionally, mothers have taken the lead on childcare while fathers have been the financial providers. Today, many U.S. families need salaries from both parents. U.S. women now have greater access to jobs.

According to the Guru Granth Sahib, the relationship between parent and child is similar to that between the creator and the creation.

69 How do families practice Sikhi together?

It is the parents' responsibility to pass on their faith. Many children are introduced to Sikhi at home and grow up hearing stories of the gurus. Sikh families also pray and worship together at the gurdwara or at home. They may also share food in community kitchens and celebrate religious holidays as a family.

70 May Sikhs date or marry outside the faith?

Sikhs are encouraged to marry within the faith. However, a person may marry outside the faith and still practice Sikhi. As with other religions and cultures in the United States, such feelings may be stronger among parents who arc more recent immigrants.

71 How do children participate in Sikhism?

Some Sikh children are brought to the gurdwara as soon as they are born. Various rites of passage, centered around the gurdwara, celebrate their growth in Sikhi.

72 Do Sikhs have generational differences?

There are differences among generations in all groups, regardless of religion. This can be especially true when accompanied by immigration and changing cultures. With technology, younger Sikhs have been able to connect with distant relatives and friends in ways their parents or grandparents could not. This connects younger Sikhs with elders and their traditions. Younger generations often have different values than their ancestors. They will combine Sikh teachings with the values of places where they live. This will manifest in different ways, whether it is using values such as seva to get involved in politics or civil rights or becoming involved in the country's culture.

Life Stages

73 What type of head covering would a child wear?

The patka, pronounced PAT-kuh, is a small turban. It is a square piece of cloth with strings to tie it. Children wear it before they transition to a turban, which is wrapped from a much longer piece of fabric. The patka keeps the hair covered securely even through physical activity.

74 Are there milestones for children?

God's ever-present influence is exhibited even as children are named. To find a name, the Guru Granth Sahib is opened to a random page. The first letter of the first word on that page becomes the first letter of the child's name. Dastar Aandhi celebrates when boys and girls transition from patka to dastar and begin tying their own turbans. This typically happens in the gurdwara under the eye of the granthi, family members or other elders. Another ritual, called Charni Lagna, marks when a child or adult develops proficiency in reading the Sikh scripture independently. One more important ceremony is the Amrith Sanchaar, the formal initiation ceremony into the Sikh faith. In it, devotees commit to living by the Rehat Maryada, practicing Sikh values and maintaining the articles of faith at all times.

75 What are Sikh weddings like?

The Sikh marriage ceremony is called the Anand Karaj. It takes place in a gurdwara. The religious part of the ceremony is less than an hour. It is a sacred commitment by the husband and wife to live a joint life centered on the guru's teachings in their pursuit of union with God. This religious ceremony includes four laavan, or verses. These show the bride and groom the path that leads to a union with God on this joint journey. The officiant is a devout Sikh who may be a man or a woman. There may have been an engagement ceremony earlier. Each family might also read the entire Guru Granth Sahib nonstop or intermittently to seek blessings for the occasion. A Sikh wedding is often a mix of faith and culture. The cultural parts of weddings vary. They can occur over several days and may reflect South Asian cultural traditions, depending on the wishes of the families. They can include singing, storytelling and henna.

76 What is the significance of an Anand Karaj wedding?

Anand Karaj means "blissful union." They are held at a congregational gathering and typically unite two Sikhs. If one of the parties is not Sikh, they may convert in advance of the wedding day. The husband and wife vow to stay faithful, as their relationship is meant to represent the love between the human soul and the supreme infinite soul.

Mantej Singh and his younger brother,
Kaviraj Singh, will one day exchange their patkas for
adult-style turbans. Photo courtesy Sharan Singh.

77 What are features of Sikh funerals?

A Sikh funeral celebrates life and recognizes that death is its natural conclusion. The soul is then free to return to God. Mourning is accepted and people provide comfort. Behavior tends not to be overly emotional. The service is usually 30-60 minutes and happens at a gurdwara with singing praises and prayer. Caskets are typically open. Cremation is preferred. At the cremation site there might be more singing, speeches and a final prayer. Families normally return to the gurdwara for the completion of an intermittent reading of the Guru Granth Sahib. Ashes are usually distributed in water. There typically are no monuments.

Persecution

78 Have Sikhs been persecuted?

Sikhs have been targeted since the religion began. Part of this has to do with their staunch commitment to opposing injustice. Another has to do with their clear identity. Two of the 10 human gurus were tortured and martyred by political authorities, as were some of their relatives. After the execution of warrior Banda Singh Bahadur in 1716, Sikhs were blamed and persecuted for an agrarian revolt. Throughout the 18th century, Persian and Afghan invaders of Punjab attacked Sikhs. Sikhs faced violence from India in the 1980s and are regularly targeted by hate in the West. Sikhi encourages people in moments of intense persecution to double down on justice.

79 Has there been a Sikh diaspora?

The 1947 partition of India pushed many Sikhs out of their homes and South Asia altogether. The partition occurred as the British Empire was leaving India after almost 200 years of colonization and rule. The partition split the country into a Hindu-majority India and the new Muslim-majority Pakistan. Millions, including Hindus, Muslims and Sikhs, were killed, kidnapped or displaced. Because the partition ran right through the Sikh homeland of Punjab, Sikhs were at the epicenter of violence and displacement. Some Sikhs stayed in Pakistan, but most wound up in India.

80 Does widespread, organized persecution continue?

Sikhs have grown up hearing how relatives and friends were forced to hide from mobs intent on killing them in 1984. That year, anti-Sikh riots followed the assassination of India's prime minister, Indira Gandhi. Before the attack, Gandhi ordered the removal of Jarnail Singh Bhindranwale, a popular Sikh political leader, from the Golden Temple. Gandhi used the paramilitary to do this. This resulted in the deaths of Bhindranwale and many followers and caused destruction at the gurdwara. Following Gandhi's assassination by two Sikh bodyguards, mobs swept through cities across India. Thousands of Sikhs were killed and 50,000 were displaced. This weighs heavily on Sikhs today, who call it genocide. Activists and organizations such as Ensaaf and Human Rights Watch assert that the Indian government has not done enough to convict the perpetrators and provide reparations to the Sikh community. The causes of the 1984 riots, its outcomes and estimates of casualties are disputed and politically controversial. The same is true of accounts about the 1947 partition of India.

81 Have Sikhs tried to have a land of their own?

According to Harvard University's Pluralism Project, yes. "The call for an independent Sikh nation, Khalistan, gained significant traction in the Sikh community both in Punjab and abroad." The Pluralism Project said U.S. Sikhs balance the issues surrounding Khalistan with maintaining their religious community in the United States.

82 Are U.S. Sikhs targeted in hate crimes?

That is increasingly true. The FBI lists Sikhs, Jews and Muslims as the most frequent subjects of religious hate crimes. U.S. Sikhs have been under attack for more than 100 years. In 1907, riots in Bellingham, Washington, and other Pacific Coast cities drove out Asian workers, primarily Sikhs. The riots led to federal anti-Asian legislation. In 1923, the Supreme Court upheld the cancellation of World War I veteran Bhagat Singh Thind's citizenship. It ruled that, although racial classifications recognized Indians as Caucasian, they were not "White" in the eyes of the "common man." In 2001, four days after the 9/11 terror attacks, a White man murdered Sikh American Balbir Singh Sodhi at his Arizona gas station. The killer was seeking to avenge the attacks by killing someone he saw as the enemy. Similar violence followed. In 2012, a White supremacist fatally shot six Sikhs and wounded four others at a gurdwara in Oak Creek, Wisconsin. One of the wounded died years later from his head wounds. In 2021 at a FedEx warehouse in Indianapolis that employed many Sikhs, a former employee killed eight people. Four were Sikhs. At a vigil after the attack, author and interfaith activist Valarie Kaur said, "Whether it was a hate crime or not, the effect was the same." The 2020 SALDEF National Sikh American Survey found that 53 percent of 1,861 respondents said they have been bullied or harassed for their identity. Additionally, 63 percent said they have been discriminated against because of their turbans.

83 Are Sikh children bullied?

According to SALDEF's 2020 survey, 67 percent of Sikh American children said their religion or traditions were not taught in school. Respondents also said their children were either the only or one of the few Sikhs in their school. The Sikh Coalition reported that the 2017-2018 school year had more school bullying complaints than the previous two years combined. The Sikh Coalition reports that boys are often bullied for wearing turbans. Girls are bullied for having long hair. The bullying report states that turbaned Sikhs face bullying at twice the national average.

84 Are Sikhs profiled?

Firsthand accounts and data indicate Sikh Americans have been increasingly profiled by law enforcement since 9/11. According to a 2009 report by the Sikh Coalition, 41 percent of Sikhs surveyed in New York City have been called names such as "Osama bin Laden" and "terrorist." Sikhs have also been profiled at airports. Hundreds have filed complaints through the Sikh Coalition's FlyRights app.

Civil Rights

85 Why are civil rights important to Sikhs?

There are several reasons. One is their religious value of equality for all. Another is their call to defend all people and uphold social justice. A third is their personal experience with injustice. Some see civil rights work as seva, an act of selfless service. Many get engaged politically or in the public sphere.

86 What are key policy issues for U.S. Sikhs?

Sikhs rank religious freedom, racial justice and healthcare as their most important political issues, in that order. About 70 percent said racial justice was the most important issue for them. Inequalities in gender and wealth are also mentioned frequently.

87 How do Sikhs view the notion of justice and equality?

Sikh scripture promotes equality and the rights of all to peace and prosperity. Scripture says God sees all people as equals. Sikhi foundations are gender equality, racial diversity, freedom of religion, service to community, equal opportunity and social justice.

88 Why do Sikhs protest India's farming laws?

In 2020, Indian farmers, predominantly from northern states including Punjab and Haryana, began protesting laws that removed protections for farmers. The laws empowered corporations to set agricultural prices. This makes it harder for small farmers to make money. Protesting farmers have met internet blackouts, arrests and water cannons. Most Sikhs live in Punjab and rely heavily on agriculture. They have been at the forefront of the protests.

89 How do Sikhs regard abortion?

There is no single Sikh perspective on ethical questions such as abortion. The Sikh Research Institute in Vancouver, Canada, issued a report in 2019. It said Sikhs "believe life begins at some time after conception, and that health issues are the number one reason that people seek abortions. The responses outlined a clear belief that Sikh institutions should play some role in providing support and resources for those considering abortion, but that ultimately the decision is the individual's alone."

Politics

90 Do Sikhs engage in politics?

According to SALDEF's 2020 opt-in survey, 96 percent of respondents said they planned to vote that year. About three-fourths said they had participated in political activities by signing online petitions in the prior 12 months. Almost two-thirds said they had donated money to campaigns or political causes.

91 How do U.S. Sikhs vote?

In the 2020 SALDEF survey, 62 percent of respondents identified as Democrats. Fifteen percent identified as independents and 7 percent identified as Republicans.

92 Do Sikhs hold U.S. political office?

Sikh doctrine supports political activity. Prominent Sikh officials have included:

Dalip Singh Saund: U.S. House of Representatives, 1957-1963. He was the first Asian American and Sikh American elected to Congress.

Ravinder Bhalla: Hoboken, New Jersey, mayor, took office in 2018.

Preet Bharara: Southern District of New York U.S. attorney, 2009-2017.

Gurpal Samra: Livingston, California, mayor, 2018-2020.

Gurbir Grewal: New Jersey attorney general, 2018-2021, then chief of enforcement at the U.S. Securities and Exchange Commission.

Preet Didbal: Yuba City, California, mayor, 2014-2018.

Manka Dhingra: Washington State senator starting in 2017.

Sikh political affiliation by region

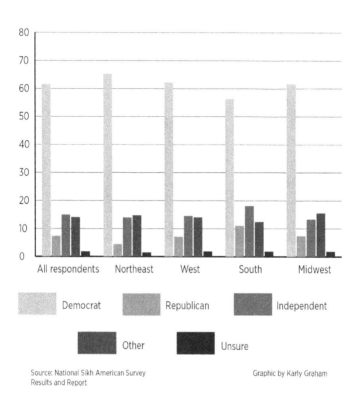

Source: National Sikh American Survey
Results and Report

Graphic by Karly Graham

Sikh activity

Respondents were asked which political activities they had done in support of a group, cause or campaign over the last 12 months.

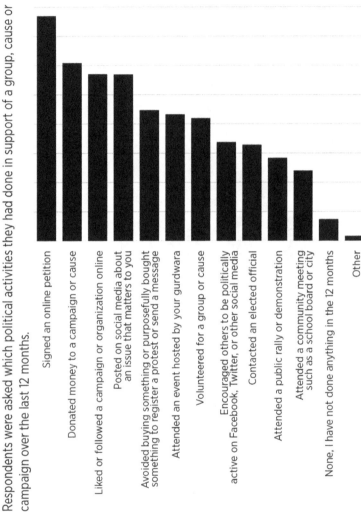

Work and Money

93 What does Sikhism teach about wealth?

Core principles emphasize a strong work ethic to make a living honestly and ethically and to share it with those in need. Attachment to wealth and acting greedy are condemned.

94 How are gurdwaras supported?

Sikh scripture encourages dasvandh and began with Guru Nanak. This means one-tenth giving. For Sikhs, this is to give a minimum of one-tenth of their earnings back to God and to the community. This can also include dedicating time and service to those in need.

95 What is the average level of education for U.S. Sikhs?

The average level of education reported for Sikhs is higher than the country's average educational level. The U.S. Census Bureau estimates that in 2020, about 36 percent of people older than 25 had a bachelor's degree or higher. The 2020 SALDEF survey reported 73.9 percent of Sikh adults had college degrees. Respondents were self-selected.

96 Do Sikhs face employment discrimination?

Sikhs have faced discrimination at work and while applying. Some Sikhs have been denied jobs because of their turbans, beards and other articles of faith. Organizations like the Sikh Coalition have won cases against employers who sought to discriminate, segregate or terminate Sikhs on the basis of religion or identity.

97 Do Sikhs serve in the military?

Yes. Sikhs have served in the U.S. military since World War I and II and still do. However, in the 1980s the U.S. Armed Forces barred articles of faith including turbans and unshorn hair. The U.S. Army and the U.S. Air Force now make religious accommodations.

Sikh household income

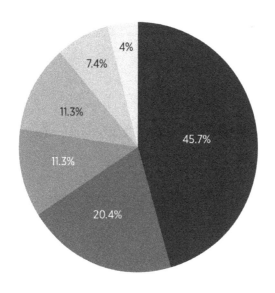

Holidays

98 What are important Sikh holidays?

Sikhs observe gurpurabs, commemorations of the birth or passing of the gurus. The gurpurab celebrating the birth of Guru Nanak Dev, the first guru, is normally celebrated in November, although there is a movement calling for it to be celebrated in April. The gurpurab celebrating the birth of Guru Gobind Singh, the tenth guru, takes place at the beginning of January. Another important January holiday is Maghi. It commemorates the 1705 fight by the Forty Liberated Ones. They died defending Guru Gobind Singh from an attack by an imperial army. Maghi is celebrated in gurdwaras with a complete recital of the Guru Granth Sahib. Hola Mohalla is a weeklong spring festival. It has daytime demonstrations of Sikh martial arts, evening worship and kirtan singing.

99 Do Sikhs celebrate Diwali?

Diwali is a religious Hindu festival and a cultural celebration. Sikhs have their own reason to celebrate this day. In 1619, the sixth guru, Guru Hargobind Sahib, was released from imprisonment during Diwali. Sikhs celebrate Bandi Chhor Divas, or Prisoner Release Day, and reflect on the values of justice, liberation and solidarity.

100 What is the significance of Vaisakhi to Sikhs?

The Vaisakhi, or Baisakhi, celebrates the spring harvest in Punjab. It is also religiously significant to Sikhs. On March 30, 1699, Guru Gobind Singh created the Khalsa identity and formalized the articles of faith.

For Discussion and Reflection

1. In many religions, faith and culture mix. Religious practices and cultural conventions co-exist and can grow from the same root. This guide describes Punjabi cultural or social practices that stand alongside Sikhi. Think about your own religious holidays. Are your holiday traditions a mix of faith and culture? Think about food traditions that go with your religious holidays. Are there cultural or family foods you associate with religious holidays? How might someone from your religion but a different culture celebrate differently?

2. When we learn about religions, it is natural to start with our own beliefs. Then, we ask how other beliefs are different or similar. What does it do to our exploration if we use our own faith as the starting point or the norm? How can we explore faiths from a place outside of our own context? Can we start from the context of the religion we are learning about?

3. Sikhs are often attacked by people who perceive them to be Muslims and therefore associate them with terrorism. What are the factors that contribute to these assumptions?

4. Many Sikhs share surnames: Singh for males, and Kaur for females. The idea was to signal equality and unity and to break from a past when someone's name indicated their station in life. How do names join or divide us?

5. In this guide, we purposely left questions about uncut hair and turbans for later. We wanted to first tell about Sikh beliefs and values. We know practices are important and interesting, but we did not want to start there. In what other religions do we see more curiosity about how people look or practice than in their beliefs? When people ask you about your faith, do they ask about practices and symbols or the reasons behind them?

6. Pronouncing "Sikh" gives non-Sikhs pause because it is properly said like "sick." That seems wrong or rude, so some people say "seek." Now, even some American Sikhs say it that way, but the "sick" pronunciation is more authentic and respectful. In what ways can pronunciation or mispronunciation interfere with our efforts to learn about each other?

7. Around the world Sikhism, or Sikhi, is practiced in the Punjabi language. Islam is rooted in Arabic. Judaism is rooted in Hebrew. What are the advantages and disadvantages of having one primary language?

8. Each Guru Granth Sahib is the same as the other copies of the scripture. There can be no variation. This is also true of the Torah, which is unrelated to Sikhism. Other religions, such as Christianity's New Testament, have several versions and interpretations. What does that say about different faiths?

9. Sometimes, people lump Sikhism, Hinduism, Buddhism and Jainism under the label "Indic" religions, meaning faiths founded in India, which was named by the British for the Indus River. These religions are not alike. These religions and some others are sometimes classified as "Eastern religions." Does classifying religions by geography help or hinder understanding?

Resources

The centerpiece of any Sikh gurdwara, or place of worship, is the Guru Granth Sahib. This collection of nearly 6,000 hymns is more than a holy book or text. It is the continuing guru of the faith and is always present for worship and major functions. The Guru Granth Sahib is covered with colorful cloth and is never left unattended in the open. In recognition of the power of books, we include this bibliography, where you may learn more. Here are some suggestions for further reading:

Dhillon, Harish. *The First Sikh Spiritual Master: Timeless Wisdom from the Life and Techniques of Guru Nanak.* Nashville: SkyLight Paths. 2006.

Fisher, Mary Pat and Robin Rinehart. *Living Religions (10th edition).* New York City: Pearson. 2016.

Hinnells, John, ed. *The Penguin Handbook of the World's Living Religions.* New York City: Penguin. 1997.

Kaur Singh, Nikky-Guninder. *First Sikh.* India: Viking 2019.

Kaur Singh, Nikky-Guninder. *Sikhism: An Introduction.* London: I.B. Tauris. 2011.

Matlins, Stuart, Arthur J. Magida, eds. *How to Be a Perfect Stranger (6th Edition): The Essential Religious Etiquette Handbook.* Nashville: Skylight Paths. 2015.

Nesbitt, Eleanor. *Sikhism: A Very Short Introduction.* Oxford: Oxford University Press. 2005.

Singh, Harbans. *The Encyclopedia of Sikhism.* New Delhi: Hemkunt Press. 2000.

Singh, Khushwant. *A History of the Sikhs, Volume 1: 1469-1839.* Oxford: Oxford India Collection. 2005.

Singh, Khushwant. *A History of the Sikhs: Volume 2: 1839-2004.* Oxford: Oxford India Collection. 2005.

Singh, Khushwant. *The Sikhs.* New York City: HarperCollins. 2008.

Singh, Mandair. *Sikhism: A Guide for the Perplexed*, illustrated. London: Bloomsbury Academic. 2013.

Singh, Patwant. *The Sikhs.* New York City: Knopf. 2000.

Singh, Simran Jeet. *The Light We Give: How Sikh Wisdom Can Transform Your Life.* New York City: Riverhead Books. 2022.

Our Story

The 100 Questions and Answers series springs from the idea that good journalism should increase cross-cultural competence and understanding. Most of our guides are created by Michigan State University journalism students.

We use journalistic interviews to surface the simple, everyday questions that people have about each other but might be afraid to ask. We use research and reporting to get the answers and then put them where people can find them, read them and learn about each other.

These cultural competence guides are meant to be conversation starters. We want people to use these guides to get some baseline understanding and to feel comfortable asking more questions. We put a resources section in every guide we make and we arrange community conversations. While the guides can answer questions in private, they are meant to spark discussions.

Making these has taught us that people are not that different from each other. People share more similarities than differences. We all want the same things for ourselves and for our families. We want to be accepted, respected and understood.

Please email your thoughts and suggestions to series editor Joe Grimm at joe.grimm@gmail.com, at the Michigan State University School of Journalism.

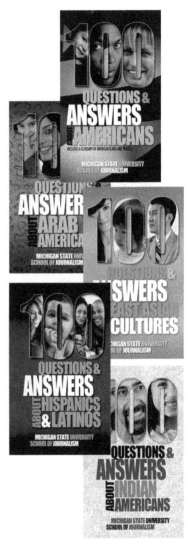

news.jrn.msu.edu/culturalcompetence

Related Books

100 Questions and Answers About Americans
Michigan State University School of Journalism, 2013

This guide answers some of the first questions asked by newcomers to the United States. Questions represent dozens of nationalities coming from Africa, Asia, Australia, Europe and North and South America. Good for international students, guests and new immigrants.

ISBN: 978-1-939880-20-8

100 Questions and Answers About Arab Americans
Michigan State University School of Journalism, 2014

The terror attacks of Sept. 11, 2001, propelled these Americans into a difficult position where they are victimized twice. The guide addresses stereotypes, bias and misinformation. Key subjects are origins, religion, language and customs. A map shows places of national origin.

ISBN: 978-1-939880-56-7

100 Questions and Answers About East Asian Cultures
Michigan State University School of Journalism, 2014

Large university enrollments from Asia prompted this guide as an aid for understanding cultural differences. The focus is on people from China, Japan, Korea and Taiwan and includes Mongolia, Hong Kong and Macau. The guide includes history, language, values, religion, foods and more.

ISBN: 978-939880-50-5

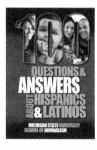

100 Questions and Answers About Hispanics & Latinos
Michigan State University School of Journalism, 2014

This group became the largest ethnic minority in the United States in 2014 and this guide answers many of the basic questions about it. Questions were suggested by Hispanics and Latinos. Includes maps and charts on origin and size of various Hispanic populations.

ISBN: 978-1-939880-44-4

Print and ebooks available on Amazon.com and other retailers.

Related Books

100 Questions and Answers About Indian Americans
Michigan State University School of Journalism, 2013

In answering questions about Indian Americans, this guide also addresses Pakistanis, Bangladeshis and others from South Asia. The guide covers religion, issues of history, colonization and national partitioning, offshoring and immigration, income, education, language and family.

ISBN: 978-1-939880-00-0 m

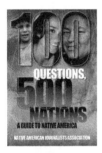

100 Questions, 500 Nations: A Guide to Native America
Michigan State University School of Journalism, 2014

This guide was created in partnership with the Native American Journalists Association. The guide covers tribal sovereignty, treaties and gaming, in addition to answers about population, religion, U.S. policies and politics. The guide includes the list of federally recognized tribes.

ISBN: 978-1-939880-38-3

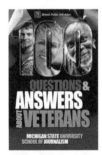

100 Questions and Answers About Veterans
Michigan State University School of Journalism, 2015

This guide treats the more than 20 million U.S. military veterans as a cultural group with distinctive training, experiences and jargon. Graphics depict attitudes, adjustment challenges, rank, income and demographics. Includes six video interviews by Detroit Public Television.

ISBN: 978-1-942011-00-2

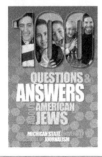

100 Questions and Answers About American Jews
Michigan State University School of Journalism, 2016

We begin by asking and answering what it means to be Jewish in America. The answers to these wide-ranging, base-level questions will ground most people and set them up for meaningful conversations with Jewish acquaintances.

ISBN: 978-1-942011-22-4

news.jrn.msu.edu/culturalcompetence

Related Books

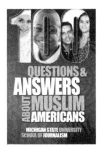

100 Questions and Answers About Muslim Americans
Michigan State University School of Journalism, 2014

This guide was done at a time of rising intolerance in the United States toward Muslims. The guide describes the presence of this religious group around the world and inside the United States. It includes audio on how to pronounce some basic Muslim words.

ISBN: 978-1-939880-79-6

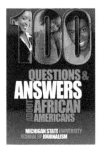

100 Questions and Answers About African Americans
Michigan State University School of Journalism, 2016

Learn about the racial issues that W.E.B. DuBois said in 1900 would be the big challenge for the 20th century. This guide explores Black and African American identity, history, language, contributions and more. Learn more about current issues in American cities and campuses.

ISBN: 978-1-942011-19-4

100 Questions and Answers About Immigrants to the U.S.
Michigan State University School of Journalism, 2016

This simple, introductory guide answers 100 of the basic questions people ask about U.S. immigrants and immigration in everyday conversation. It has answers about identity, language, religion, culture, customs, social norms, economics, politics, education, work, families and food.

ISBN: 978-1-934879-63-4

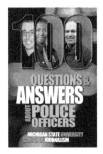

100 Questions and Answers about Police Officers
Michigan State University School of Journalism, 2018

This simple, introductory guide answers 100 of the basic questions people ask about police officers, sheriff's deputies, public safety officers and tribal police. It focuses on policing at the local level, where procedures vary from coast to coast. The guide includes a resource about traffic stops.

ISBN: 978-1-64180-013-6

Print and ebooks available on Amazon.com and other retailers.

Related Books

100 Questions and Answers About Gender Identity
Michigan State University School of Journalism, 2017

The guide is written for anyone who wants quick answers to basic, introductory questions about transgender people. It is a starting point people who want to get a fast grounding in the facts.

ISBN: 978-1-641800-02-0

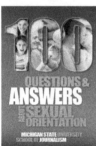

100 Questions and Answers About Sexual Orientation
Michigan State University School of Journalism, 2018

This clear, introductory guide answers 100 of the basic questions people ask about people who are lesbian, gay, bisexual or who have other sexual orientations. The questions come from interviews with people who say these are issues they frequently get asked about or wish people knew more about.

ISBN: 978-1-641800-27-3

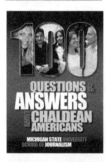

100 Questions and Answers About Chaldean Americans
Michigan State University School of Journalism, 2019

This guide has sections on identity, language, religion, culture, customs, social norms, economics, politics, education, work, families and food. It is written for those who want authoritative answers to basic, questions about this immigrant group from Iraq.

ISBN: 978-1-934879-63-4

100 Questions and Answers About Gen X Plus
100 Questions and Answers About Millennials
Michigan State University School of Journalism, 2019

This is a double guide in the Bias Busters series. It is written for those who want authoritative answers about these important generations and how we all work together.

ISBN: 978-1-641800-47-1

Related Books

True Border: 100 Questions and Answers About the U.S.-Mexico Frontera
Borderzine: Reporting Across Fronteras, 2020

This guide was developed by the University of Texas/ Borderzine for the Bias Busters cultural competence series. The guide is written for people who want authoritative answers about the U.S.-Mexico border region and get up to speed quickly on this important topic.

ISBN: 978-1-641800-60-0

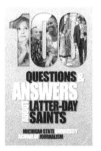

100 Questions and Answers About Latter-day Saints
Michigan State University School of Journalism, 2020

The guide is written for those who want authoritative answers to basic questions about the Latter-day Saints faith. It relies extensively on the Church of Jesus Christ of Latter-day Saints writings and suggests resources for greater depth.

ISBN: 978-1-641800-90-7

Print and ebooks available on Amazon.com and other retailers.

CPSIA information can be obtained
at www.ICGtesting.com
Printed in the USA
BVHW070019100622
639357BV00005B/17